GRAPHIC SCIENCE

THE **POWERFUL WORLD** OF

ENERGY

WITH **MAX AXIOM**
SUPER SCIENTIST

by Agnieszka Biskup
illustrated by Cynthia Martin and Anne Timmons

Consultant:
Christopher J. Conklin
Chemist, Aldrich Chemical
Member, American Chemical Society
Washington, D.C.

Capstone
press®
Mankato, Minnesota

Graphic Library is published by Capstone Press,
151 Good Counsel Drive, P.O. Box 669, Mankato, Minnesota 56002.
www.capstonepress.com

Printed in the United States of America

1 2 3 4 5 6 14 13 12 11 10 09

Library of Congress Cataloging-in-Publication Data
Biskup, Agnieszka.
The powerful world of energy with Max Axiom, super scientist / by Agnieszka Biskup; illustrated by Cynthia Martin and Anne Timmons.
p. cm. — (Graphic library. Graphic science)
Includes bibliographical references and index.
Summary: "In graphic novel format, follows the adventures of Max Axiom as he explains the science behind energy" — Provided by publisher.
ISBN-13: 978-1-4296-2337-7 (hardcover)
ISBN-10: 1-4296-2337-3 (hardcover)
ISBN-13: 978-1-4296-3450-2 (softcover pbk.)
ISBN-10: 1-4296-3450-2 (softcover pbk.)
1. Force and energy — Juvenile literature. 2. Motion — Juvenile literature. 3. Adventure stories. I. Martin, Cynthia, 1961– ill. II. Timmons, Anne, ill. III. Title. IV. Series.
QC73.4.B49 2009
531'.6 — dc22 2008029651

Set Designer
Bob Lentz

Book Designer
Alison Thiele

Cover Artist
Tod G. Smith

Colorist
Krista Ward

Editor
Christopher L. Harbo

Photo illustration credits: Shutterstock/Martin D. Vonka, 23

TABLE OF CONTENTS

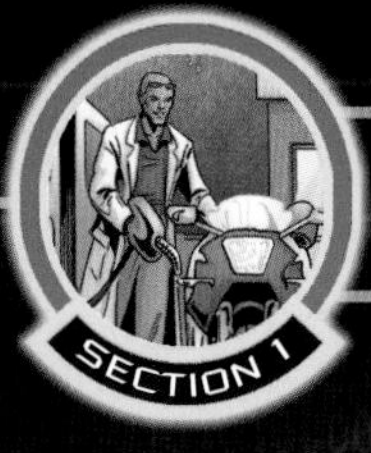
SECTION 1

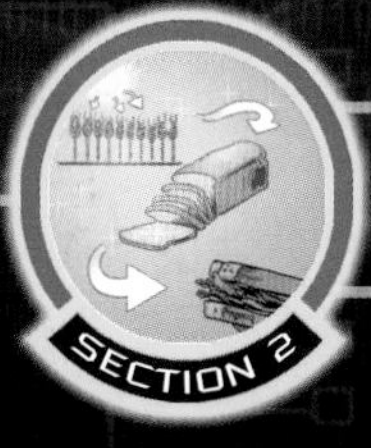
SECTION 2

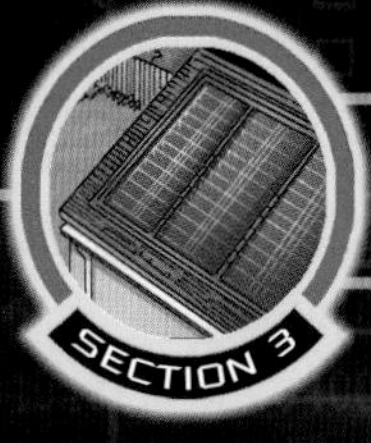
SECTION 3

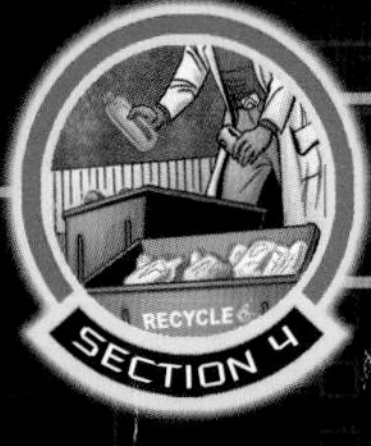
RECYCLE
SECTION 4

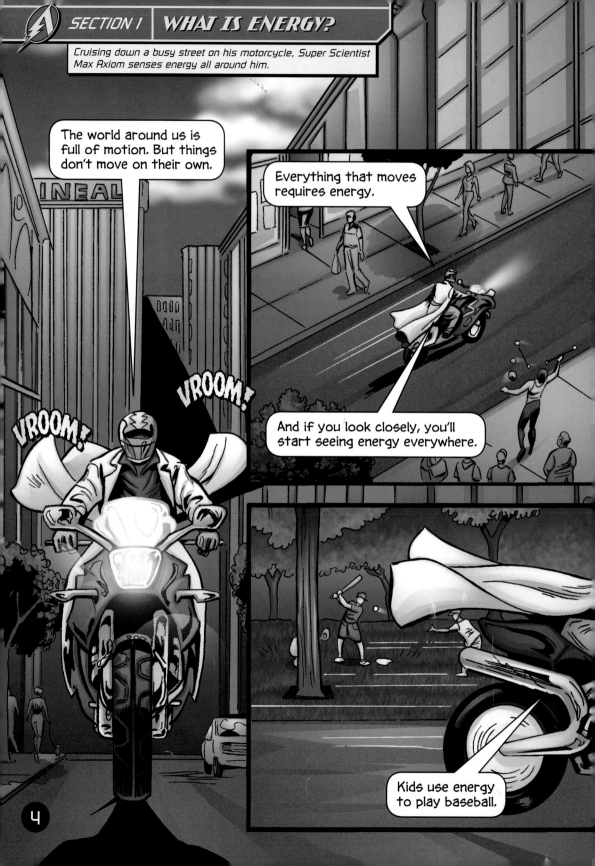

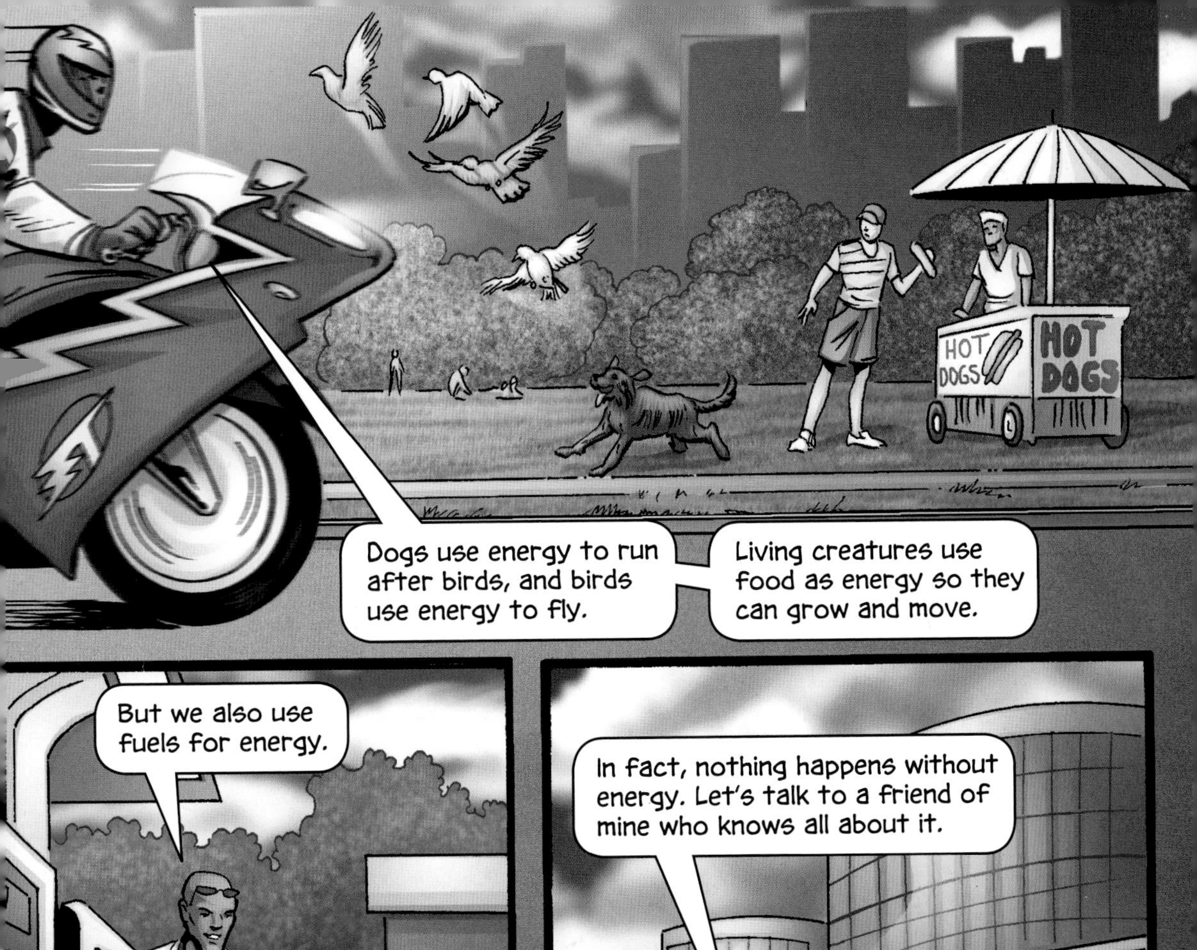
HOT DOGS
HOT DOGS
Dogs use energy to run after birds, and birds use energy to fly.
Living creatures use food as energy so they can grow and move.
But we also use fuels for energy.
Gasoline powers motorcycles, cars, and trucks.
In fact, nothing happens without energy. Let's talk to a friend of mine who knows all about it.
DEPARTMENT OF ENERGY

ENERGY AND WORK

Scientists define energy as the ability to do work. Scientists also have a specific definition for work. Work is motion against resistance. For example, lifting a book up in the air against the pull of gravity is work.

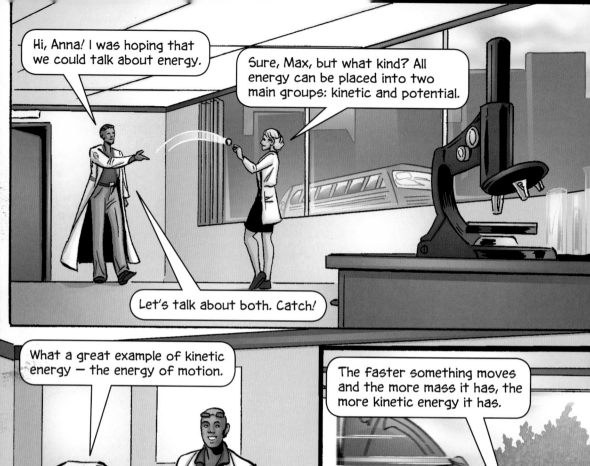

Hi, Anna! I was hoping that we could talk about energy.

Sure, Max, but what kind? All energy can be placed into two main groups: kinetic and potential.

Let's talk about both. Catch!

What a great example of kinetic energy — the energy of motion.

That's right. Anything that moves has kinetic energy. Throwing a ball or walking across the room are good examples.

The faster something moves and the more mass it has, the more kinetic energy it has.

Look at that truck. It has a lot more kinetic energy than you do because of its large mass and speed.

⚡ MASS AND MATTER

Mass is the amount of matter that makes up an object. Matter is something that takes up space. For example, a truck has more mass than a person does.

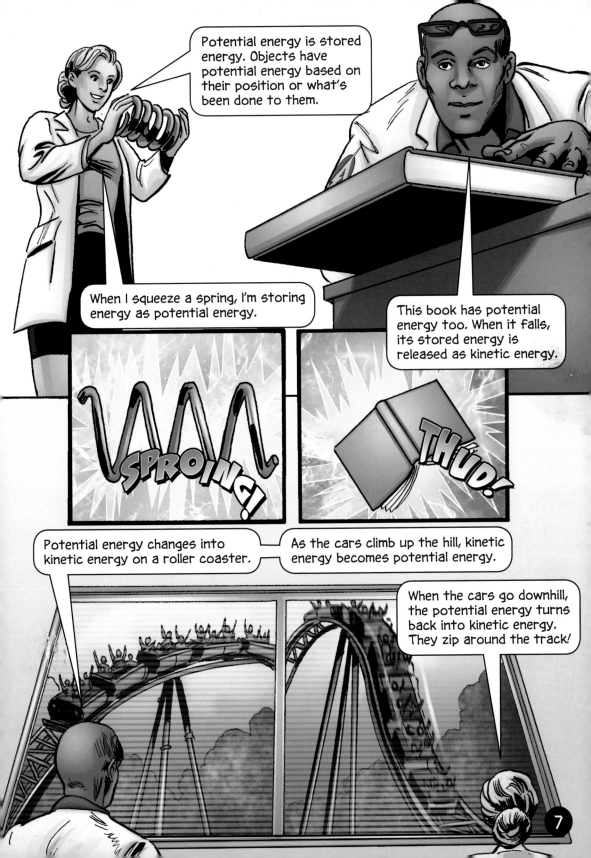

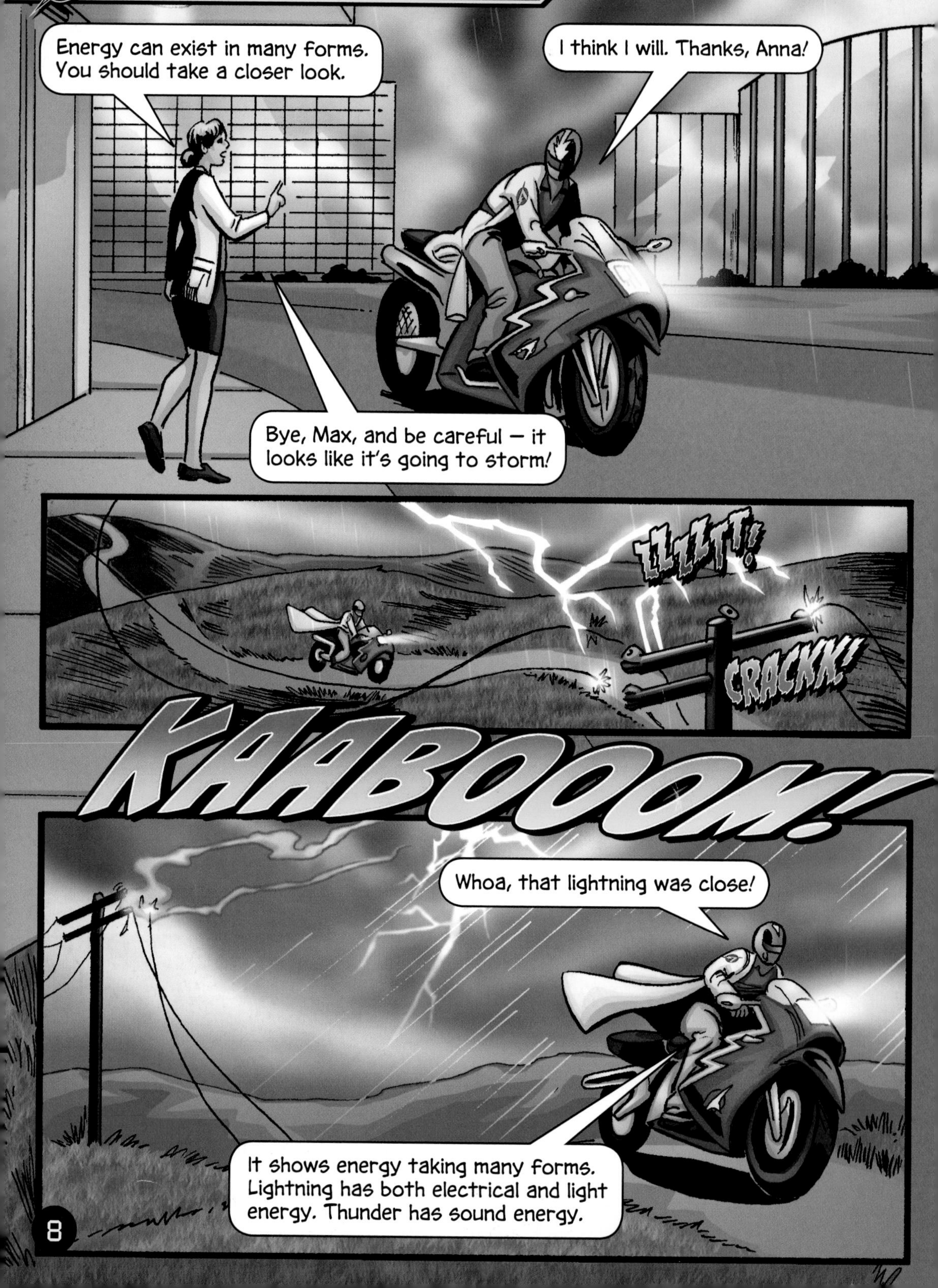
Energy can exist in many forms. You should take a closer look.
I think I will. Thanks, Anna!
Bye, Max, and be careful — it looks like it's going to storm!
ZZZZTT!
CRACKK!
KAABOOOM!
Whoa, that lightning was close!
It shows energy taking many forms. Lightning has both electrical and light energy. Thunder has sound energy.

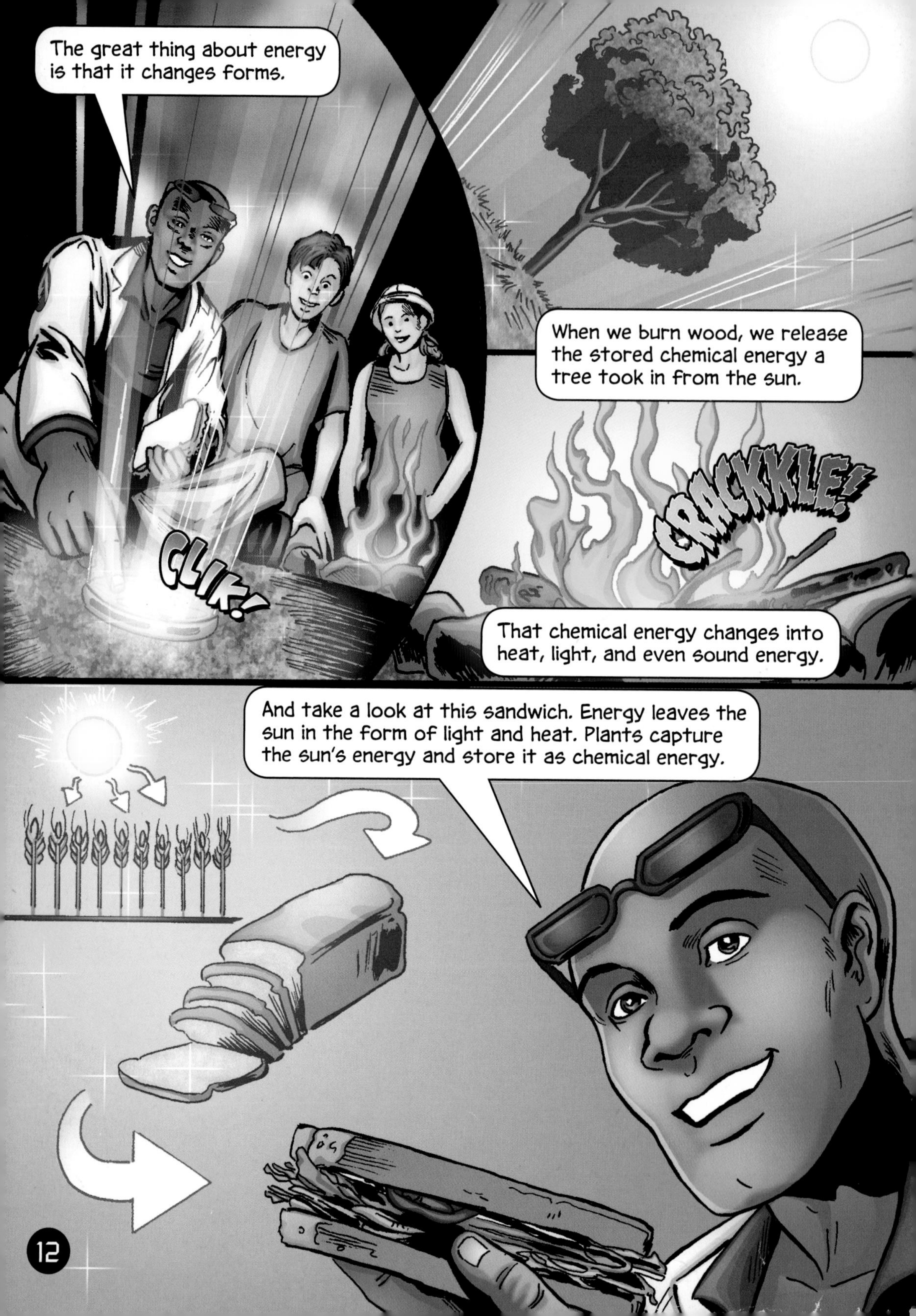

The great thing about energy is that it changes forms.
CLIK!
When we burn wood, we release the stored chemical energy a tree took in from the sun.
CRACKKLE!
That chemical energy changes into heat, light, and even sound energy.
And take a look at this sandwich. Energy leaves the sun in the form of light and heat. Plants capture the sun's energy and store it as chemical energy.

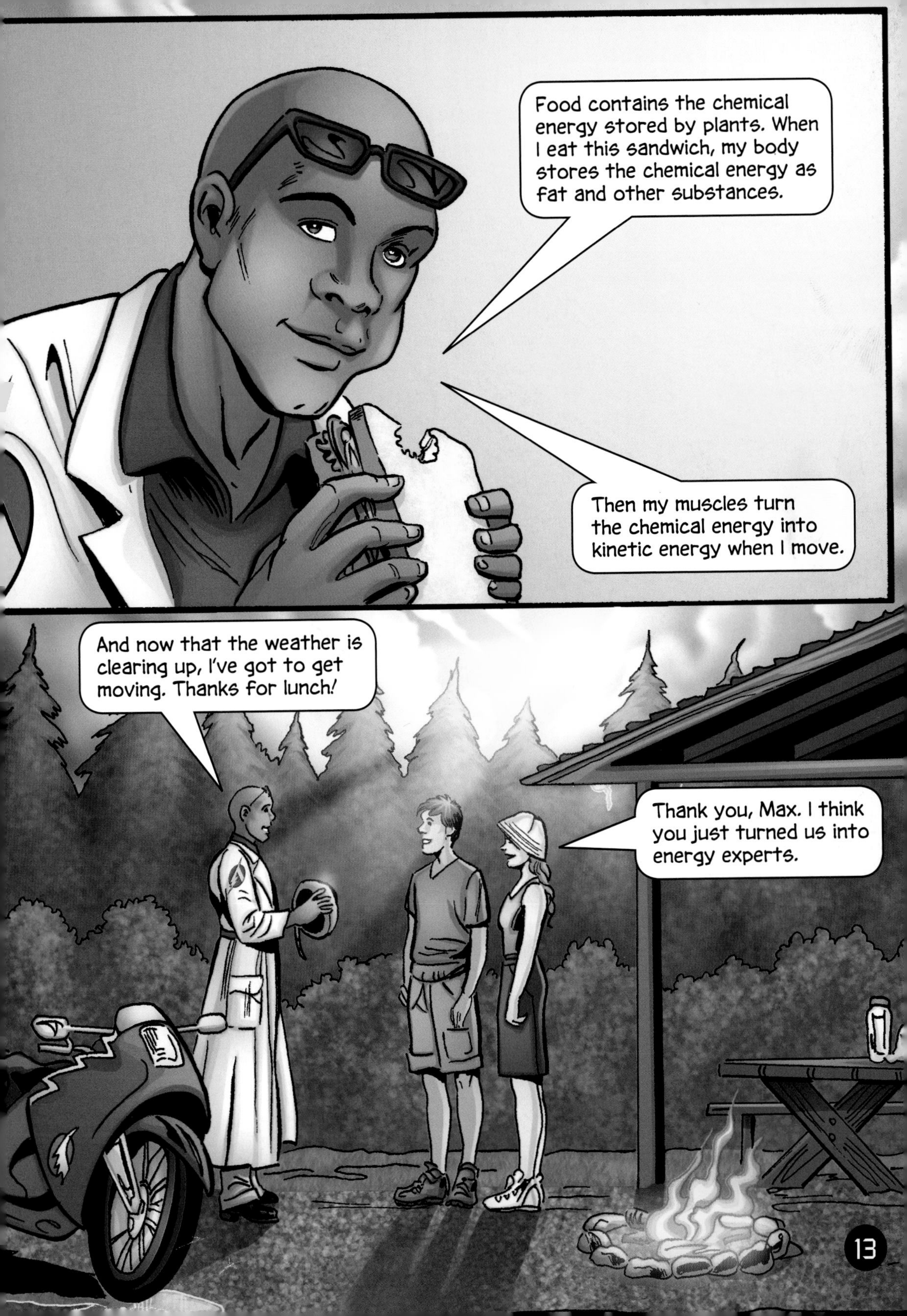
Food contains the chemical energy stored by plants. When I eat this sandwich, my body stores the chemical energy as fat and other substances.
Then my muscles turn the chemical energy into kinetic energy when I move.
And now that the weather is clearing up, I've got to get moving. Thanks for lunch!
Thank you, Max. I think you just turned us into energy experts.

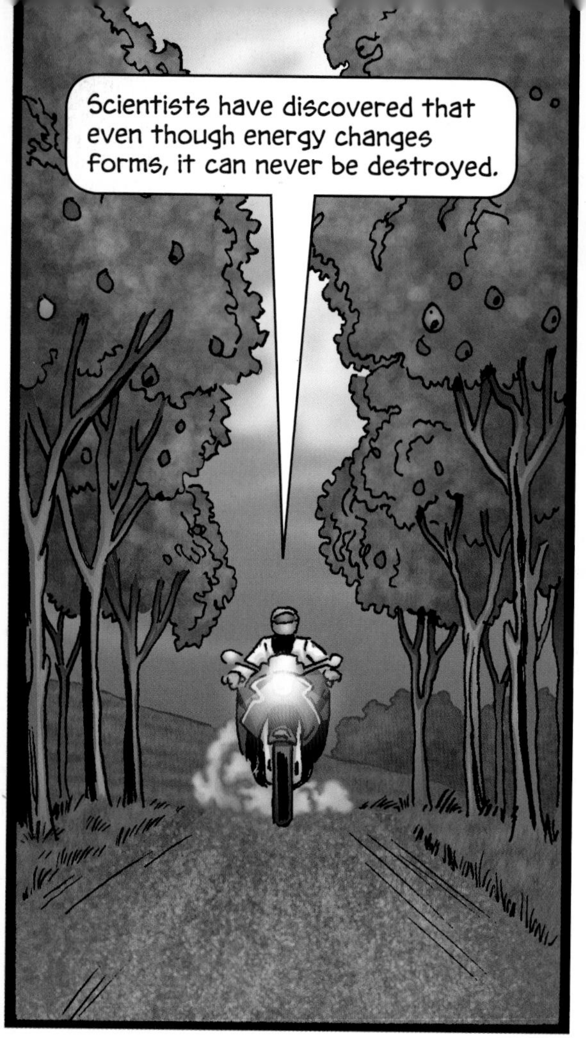
Scientists have discovered that even though energy changes forms, it can never be destroyed.

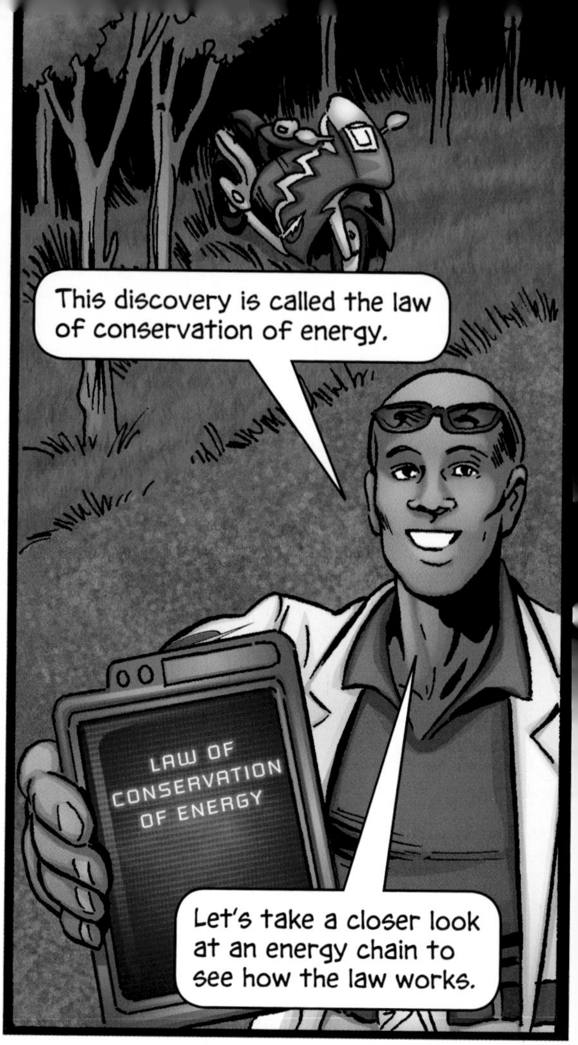
This discovery is called the law of conservation of energy.
LAW OF CONSERVATION OF ENERGY
Let's take a closer look at an energy chain to see how the law works.

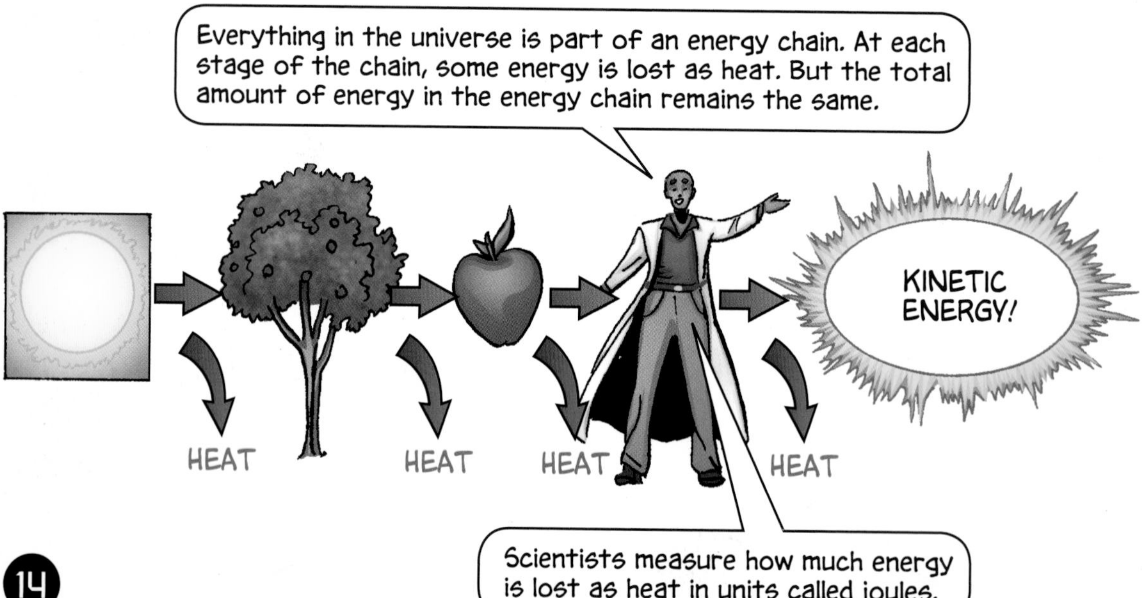
Everything in the universe is part of an energy chain. At each stage of the chain, some energy is lost as heat. But the total amount of energy in the energy chain remains the same.
KINETIC ENERGY!
HEAT
HEAT
HEAT
HEAT
Scientists measure how much energy is lost as heat in units called joules.

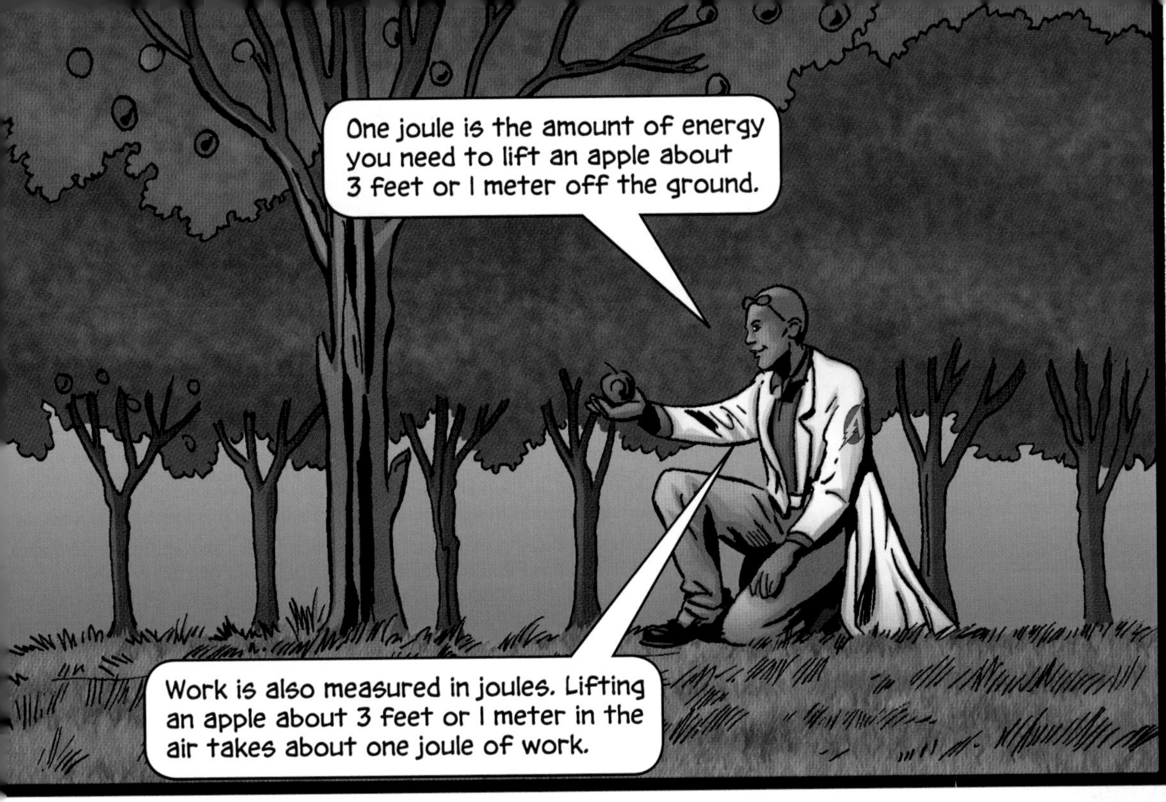
One joule is the amount of energy you need to lift an apple about 3 feet or 1 meter off the ground.
Work is also measured in joules. Lifting an apple about 3 feet or 1 meter in the air takes about one joule of work.

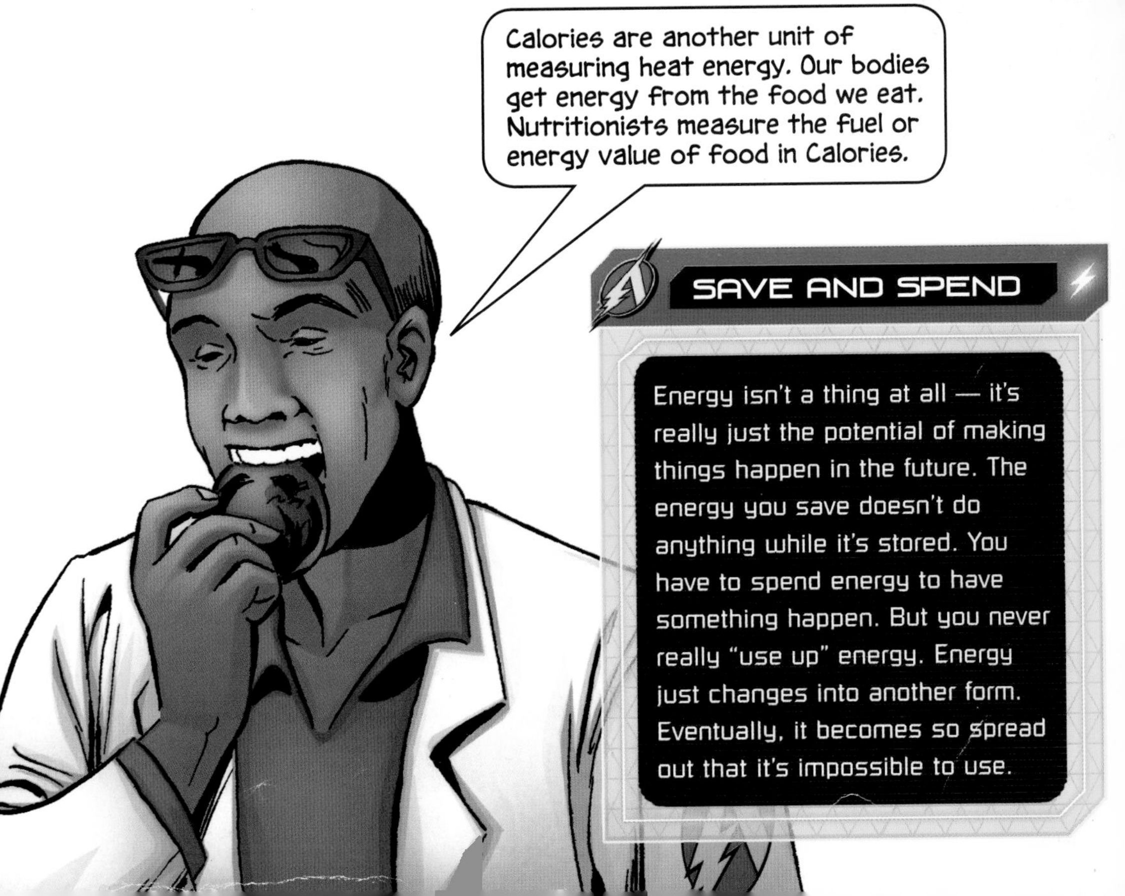
Calories are another unit of measuring heat energy. Our bodies get energy from the food we eat. Nutritionists measure the fuel or energy value of food in Calories.

SAVE AND SPEND

Energy isn't a thing at all — it's really just the potential of making things happen in the future. The energy you save doesn't do anything while it's stored. You have to spend energy to have something happen. But you never really "use up" energy. Energy just changes into another form. Eventually, it becomes so spread out that it's impossible to use.

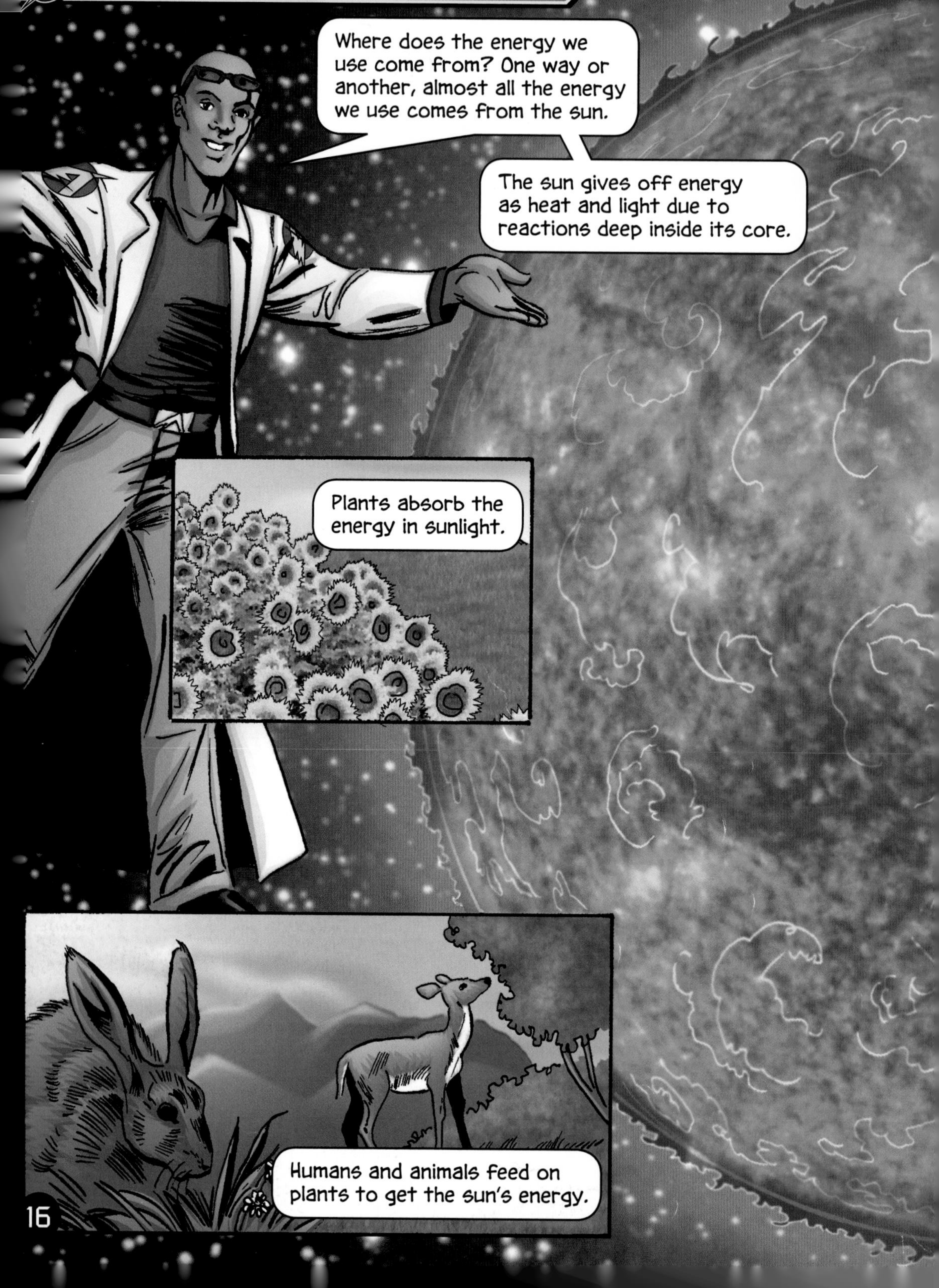
Where does the energy we use come from? One way or another, almost all the energy we use comes from the sun.
The sun gives off energy as heat and light due to reactions deep inside its core.
Plants absorb the energy in sunlight.
Humans and animals feed on plants to get the sun's energy.

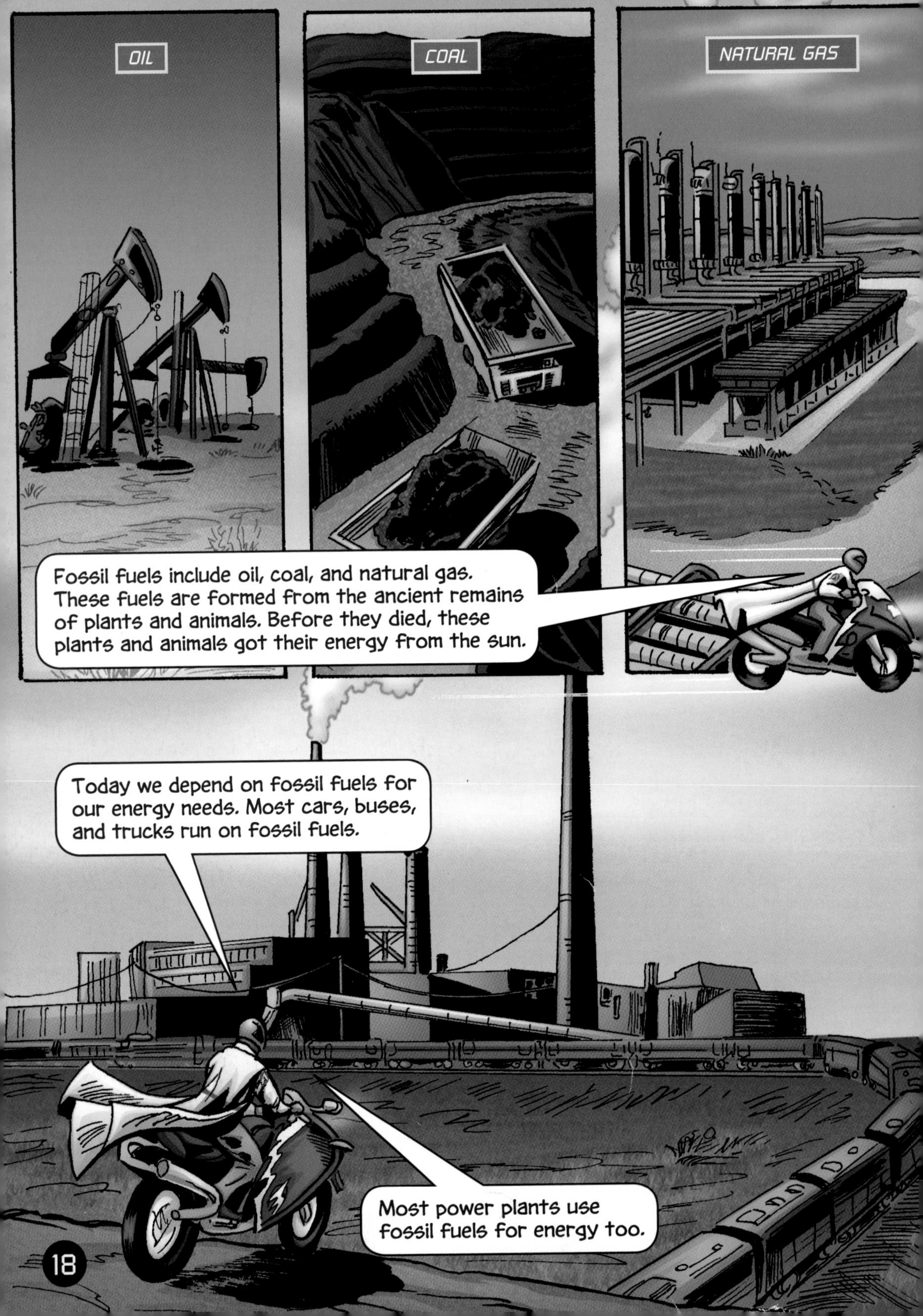
OIL
COAL
NATURAL GAS
Fossil fuels include oil, coal, and natural gas. These fuels are formed from the ancient remains of plants and animals. Before they died, these plants and animals got their energy from the sun.
Today we depend on fossil fuels for our energy needs. Most cars, buses, and trucks run on fossil fuels.
Most power plants use fossil fuels for energy too.

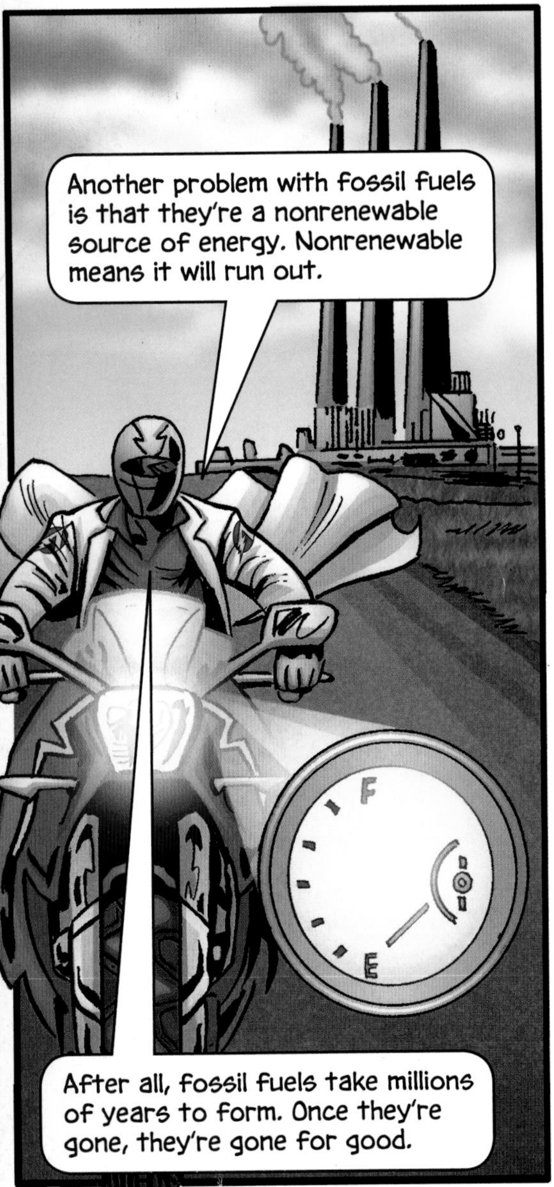
Another problem with fossil fuels is that they're a nonrenewable source of energy. Nonrenewable means it will run out.
After all, fossil fuels take millions of years to form. Once they're gone, they're gone for good.
F
E

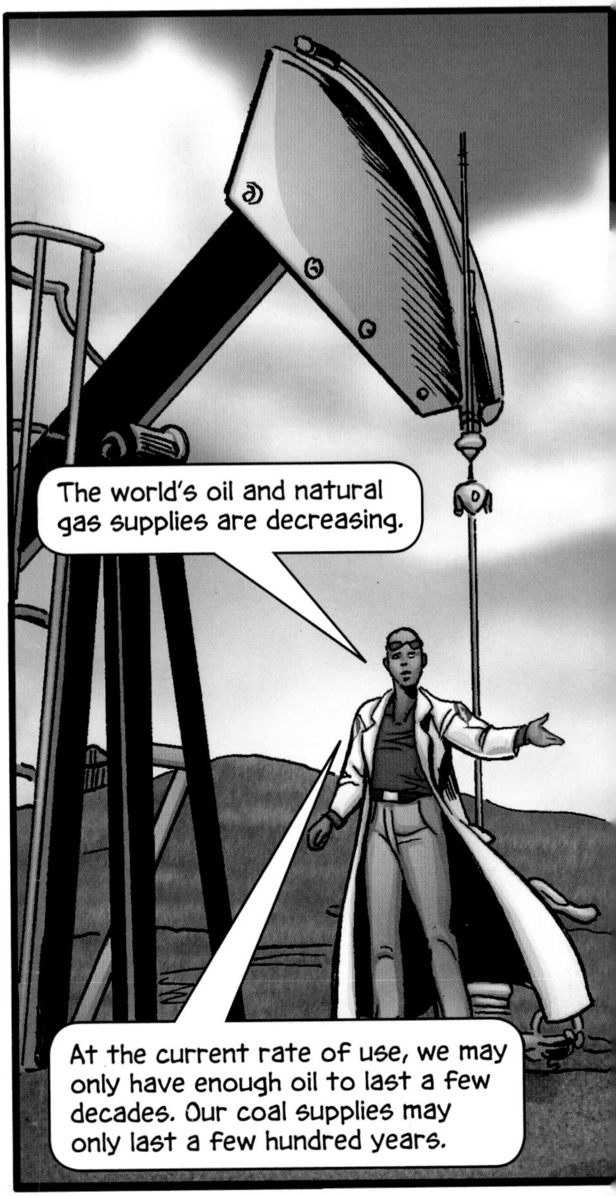
The world's oil and natural gas supplies are decreasing.
At the current rate of use, we may only have enough oil to last a few decades. Our coal supplies may only last a few hundred years.

BURNING OIL

ACCESS GRANTED: MAX AXIOM

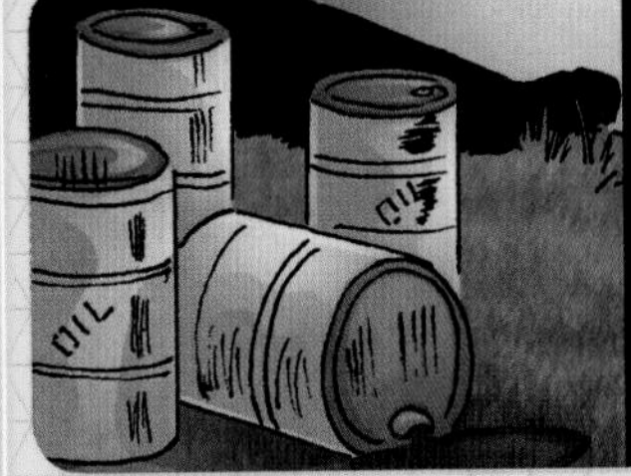
OIL
OIL

Oil is one of the most important sources of energy in the world. Refineries make oil into gasoline for our cars and jet fuel for our planes. Oil is even used in products such as crayons, tires, and dishwashing liquid. In fact, the United States uses about 20 million barrels of oil every day.

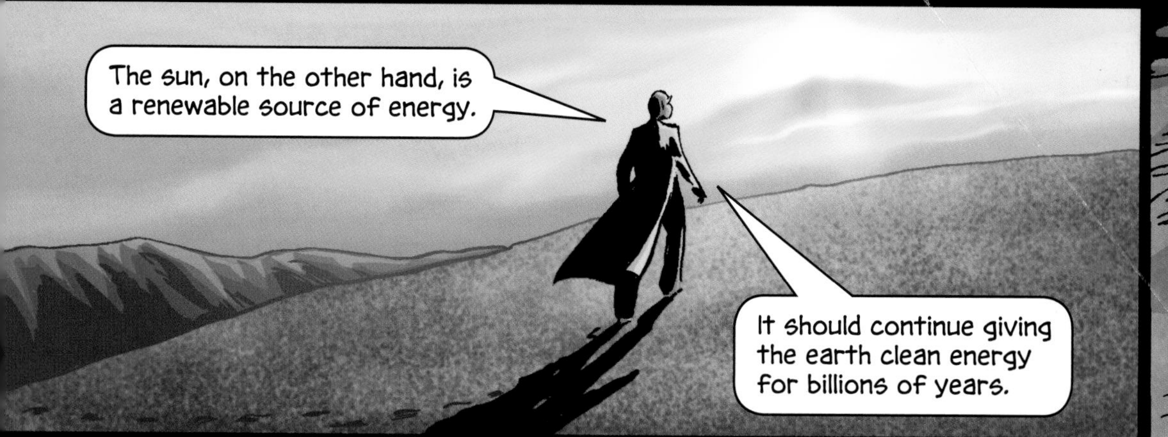
The sun, on the other hand, is a renewable source of energy.
It should continue giving the earth clean energy for billions of years.
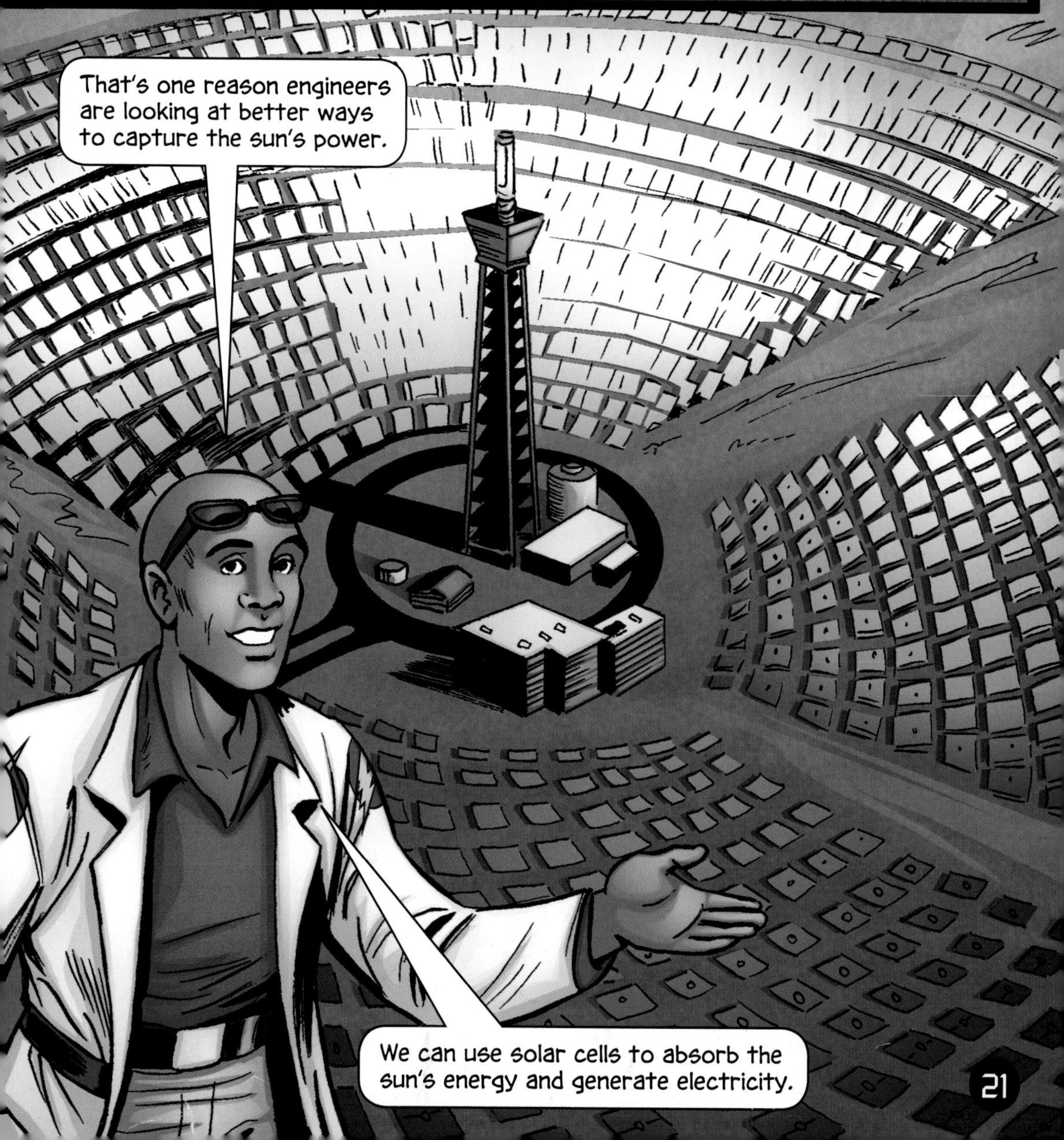
That's one reason engineers are looking at better ways to capture the sun's power.
We can use solar cells to absorb the sun's energy and generate electricity.

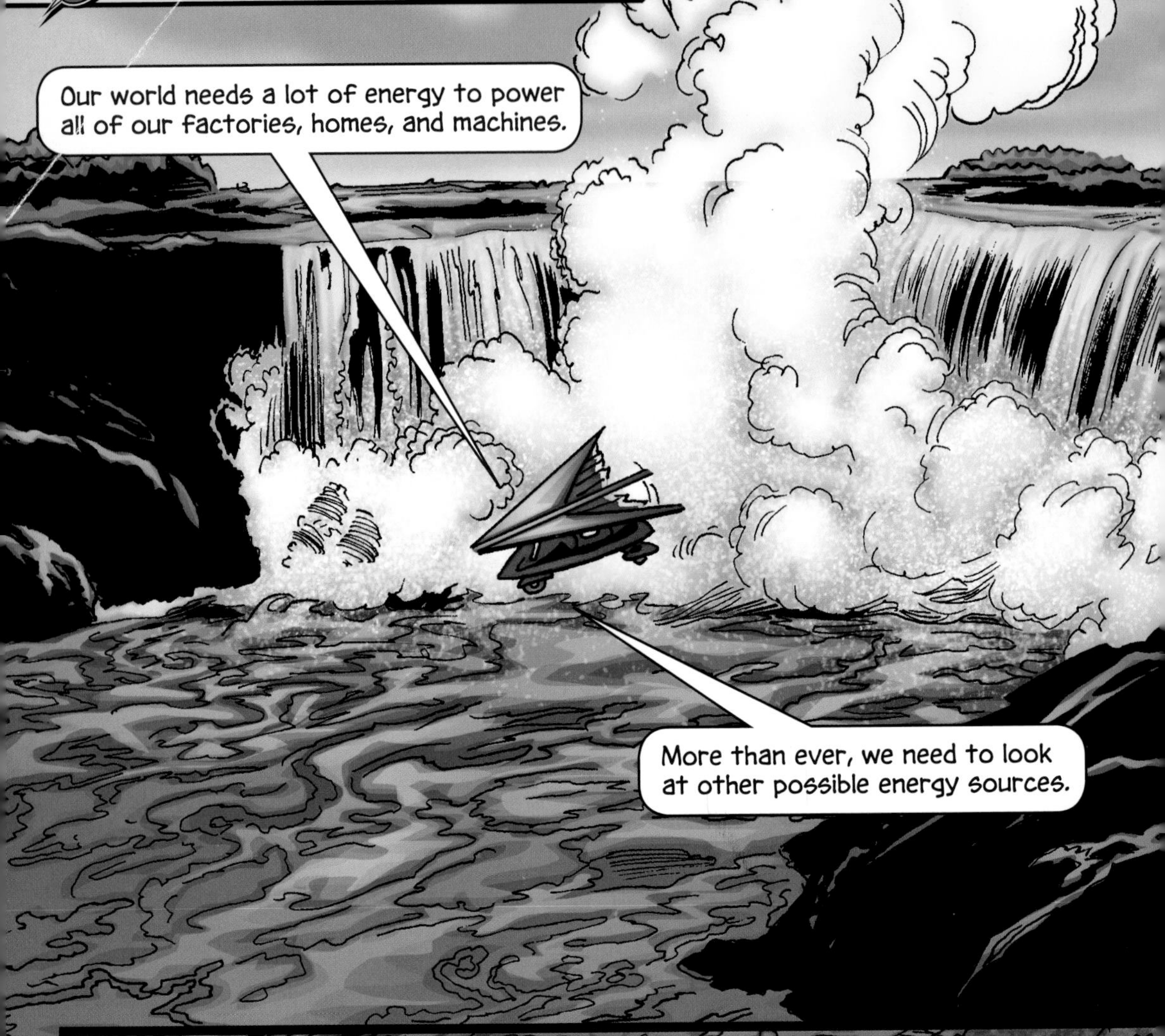
Our world needs a lot of energy to power all of our factories, homes, and machines.
More than ever, we need to look at other possible energy sources.

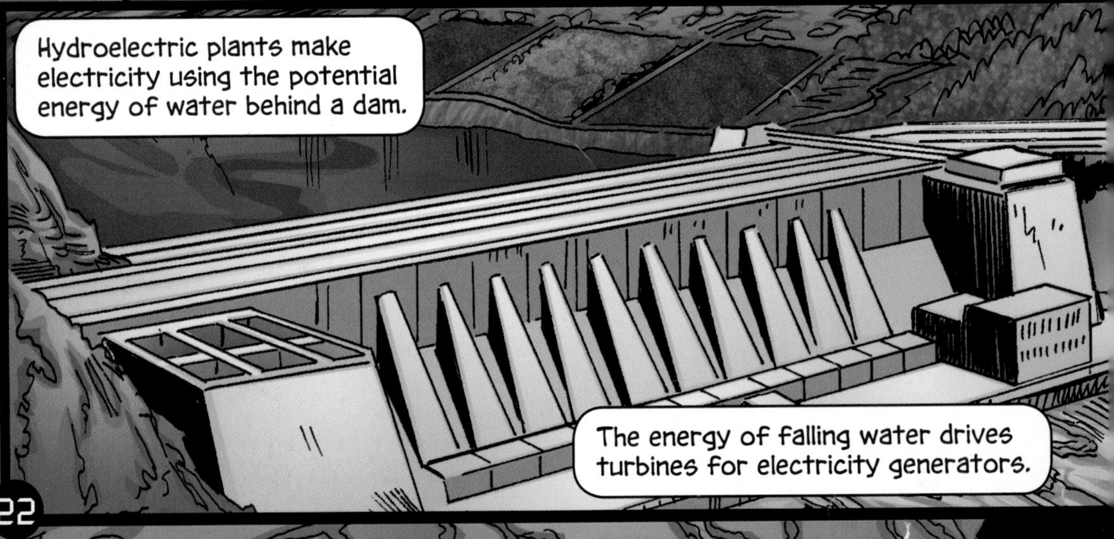
Hydroelectric plants make electricity using the potential energy of water behind a dam.
The energy of falling water drives turbines for electricity generators.

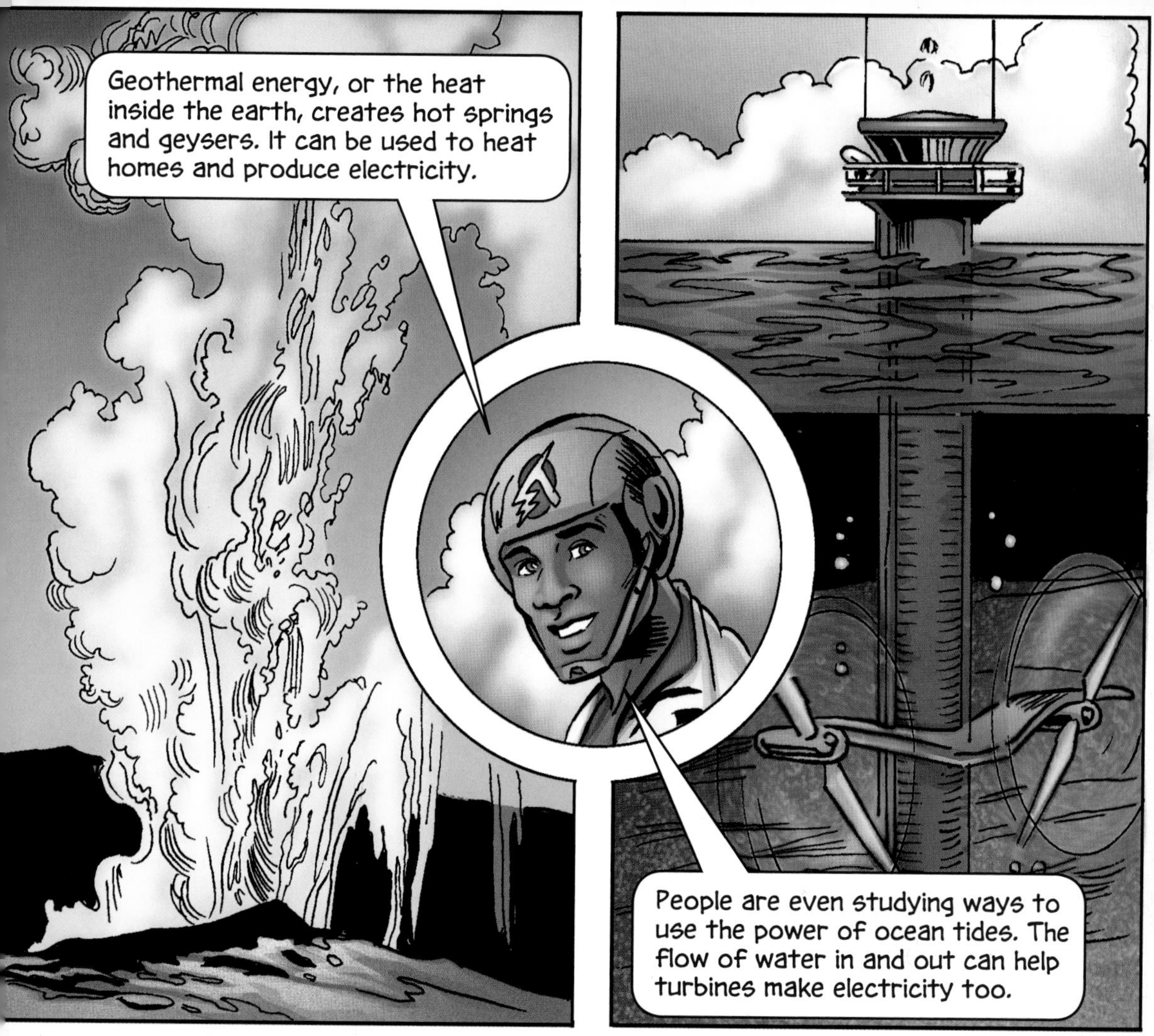
Geothermal energy, or the heat inside the earth, creates hot springs and geysers. It can be used to heat homes and produce electricity.
People are even studying ways to use the power of ocean tides. The flow of water in and out can help turbines make electricity too.

NUCLEAR POWER

ACCESS GRANTED: MAX AXIOM

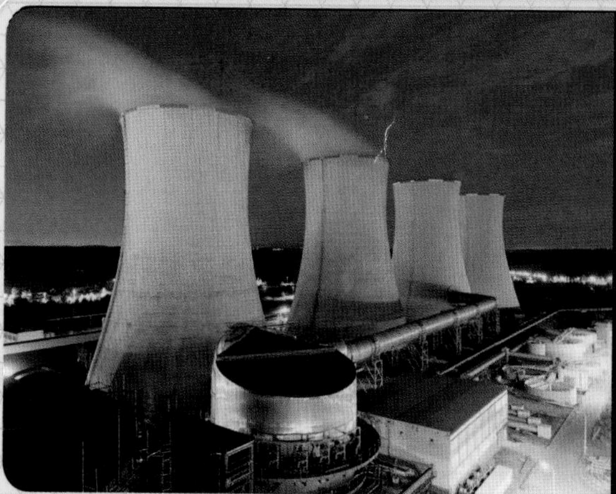

In nuclear power plants, a nuclear reactor splits atoms to generate heat. This heat turns water into steam. The steam drives turbines to produce electricity. Although nuclear power plants don't create pollutants like carbon dioxide, they do generate radioactive waste. Radiation from this waste has harmful long-term effects on people's health and the environment.

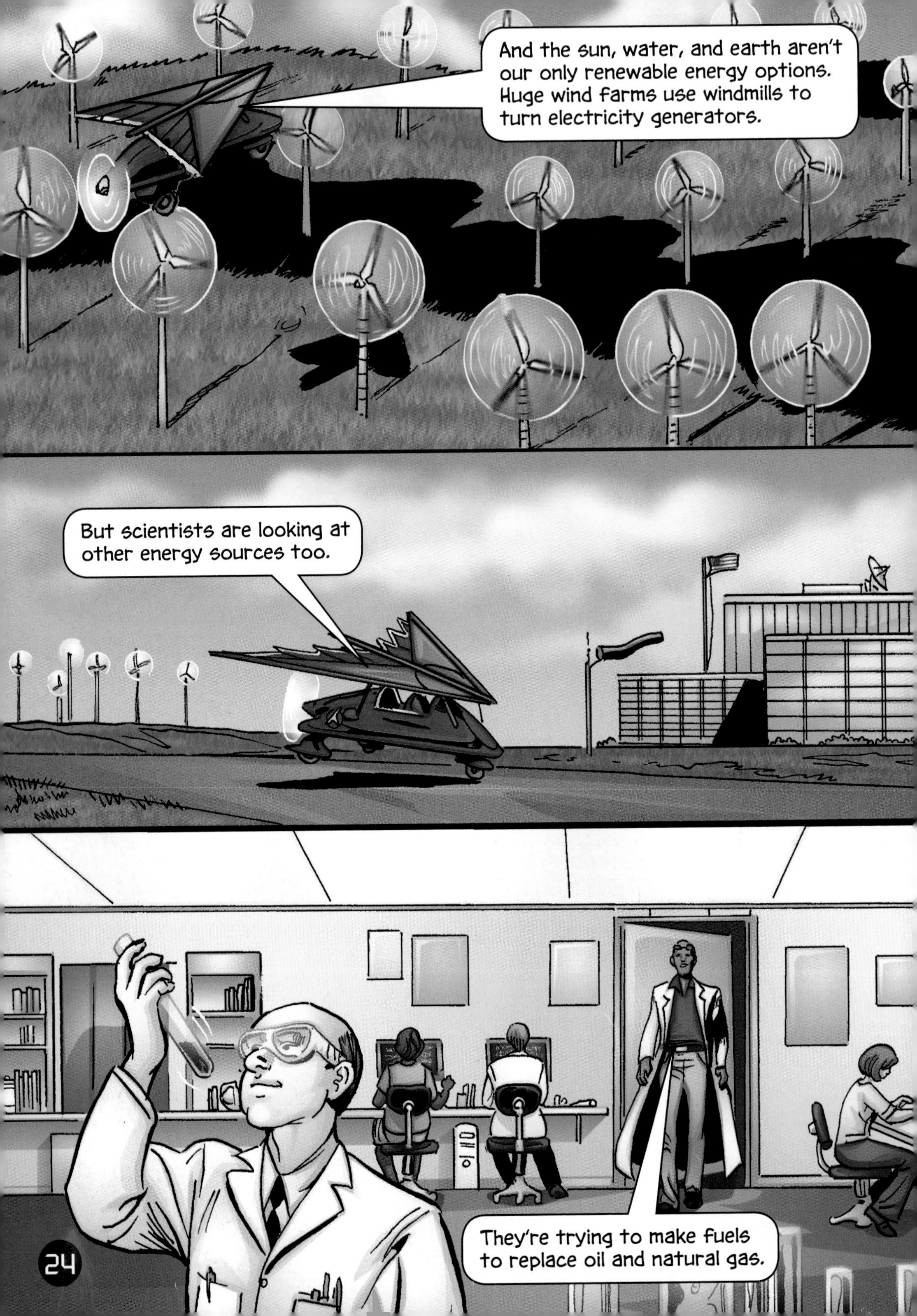

And the sun, water, and earth aren't our only renewable energy options. Huge wind farms use windmills to turn electricity generators.
But scientists are looking at other energy sources too.
They're trying to make fuels to replace oil and natural gas.

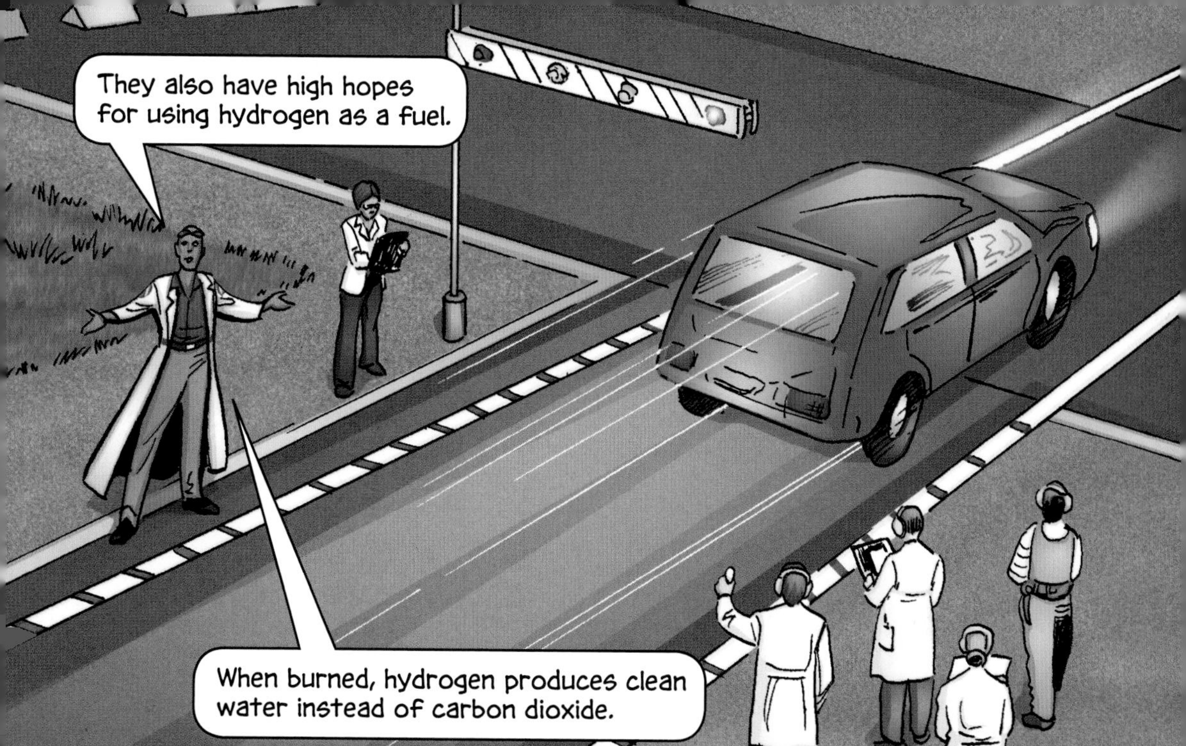
They also have high hopes for using hydrogen as a fuel.
When burned, hydrogen produces clean water instead of carbon dioxide.

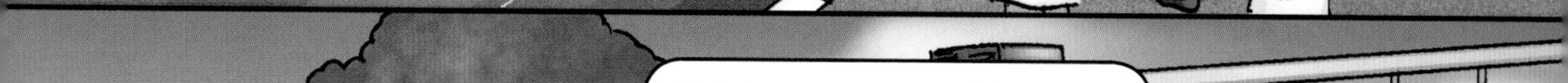
Right now, one problem is producing enough hydrogen cheaply and easily.

ETHANOL

ACCESS GRANTED: MAX AXIOM

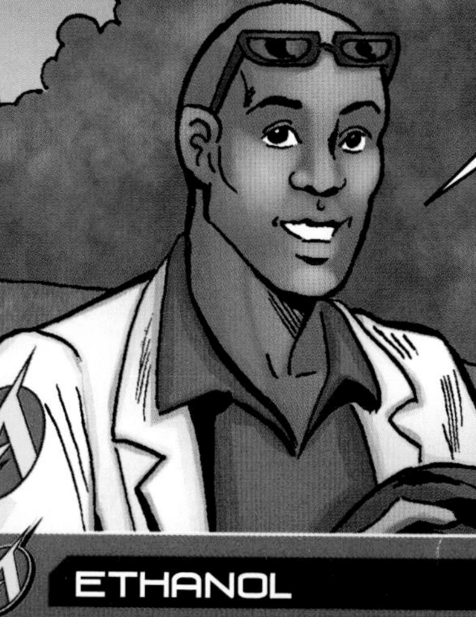

Ethanol is a renewable fuel made from plants such as corn and switch grass. Ethanol is used as an additive in gasoline. It is gaining popularity as an alternative fuel for vehicles. Researchers are trying to develop cost-effective and environmentally-friendly ways to use plants as fuels.

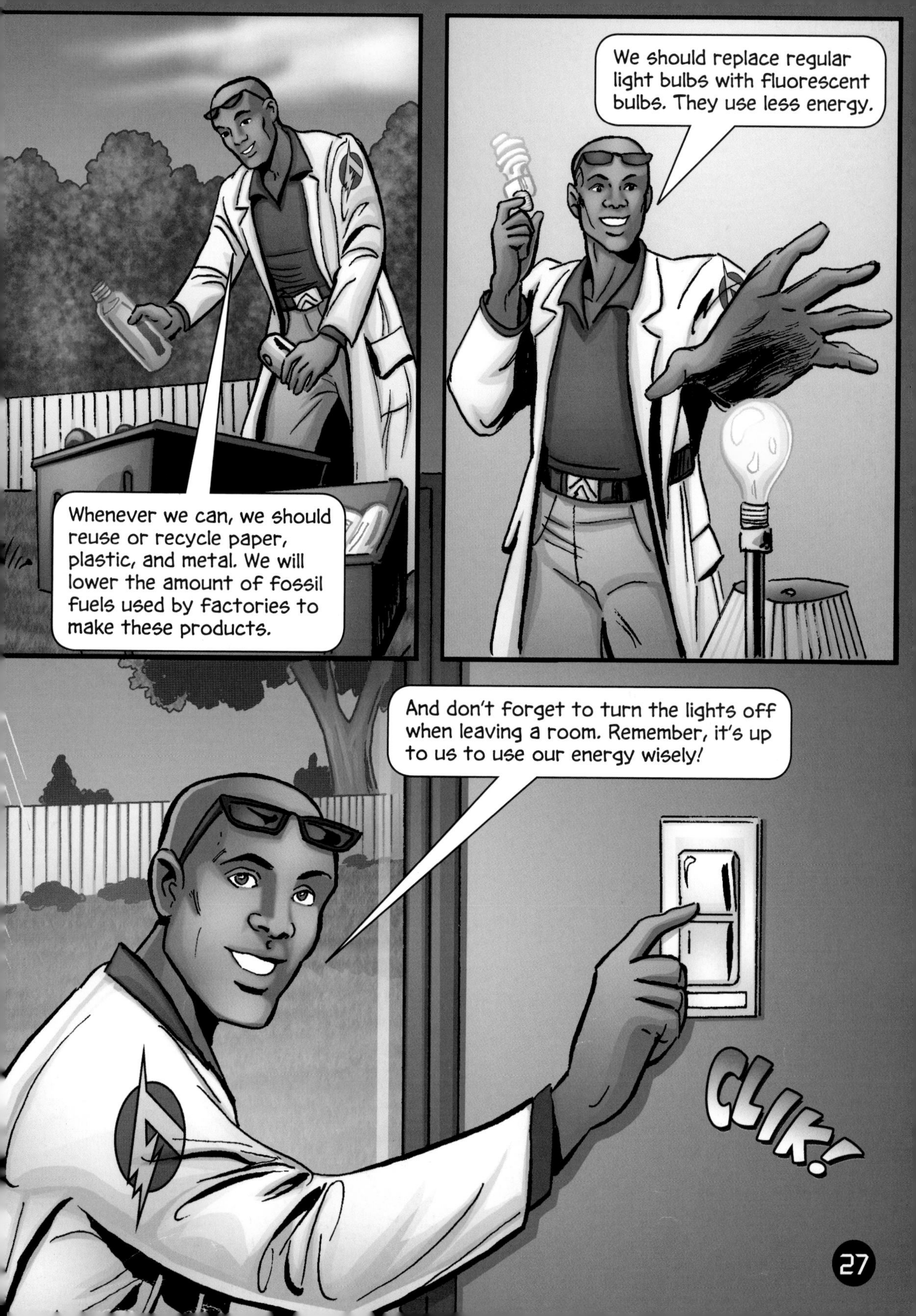
Whenever we can, we should reuse or recycle paper, plastic, and metal. We will lower the amount of fossil fuels used by factories to make these products.
We should replace regular light bulbs with fluorescent bulbs. They use less energy.
And don't forget to turn the lights off when leaving a room. Remember, it's up to us to use our energy wisely!
CLIK!

MORE ABOUT ENERGY

 Fire was probably the first great energy invention. For thousands of years, people burned wood as their main source of fuel for heat, cooking, and other uses.

 There is a whole family of energy called electromagnetic radiation. It includes gamma rays, x-rays, ultraviolet light, visible light, infrared light, microwaves, and radio waves. Visible light, however, is the only form we can see with our eyes. Some animals, like bees, can see ultraviolet light too.

 The color of light we see gives us information about its energy level. A rainbow's colors are always in the same order: red, orange, yellow, green, blue, indigo, and violet. The colors are also arranged in order of increasing energy. Red light has lower energy than green light. And violet light has the highest energy of all visible light.

 Even though we can't see x-rays, we can use them to take images of the insides of our bodies. X-rays allow us to see beneath the skin down to our bones.

 Nothing in the universe can move faster than light. Light moves at a blistering 186,000 miles (300,000 kilometers) per second. A beam of light can travel around the world seven times in just one second.

 Some scientists think the universe is filled with an invisible and mysterious force called dark energy. They believe dark energy is causing the universe to expand at an accelerating rate.

A huge amount of energy holds atoms together. In nuclear power plants, energy is released when atoms are split apart to create smaller atoms. This is called nuclear fission. In the sun, energy is produced when atoms are combined, or fused, together. This process is called nuclear fusion.

 Almost half of the energy consumed by Americans in their homes is used for space heating. Another quarter is used for lighting and appliances. The rest is used for refrigeration, air conditioning, and heating water.

MORE ABOUT

SUPER SCIENTIST

Real name: Maxwell J. Axiom
Hometown: Seattle, Washington
Height: 6' 1"   Weight: 192 lbs
Eyes: Brown   Hair: None

Super capabilities: Super intelligence; able to shrink to the size of an atom; sunglasses give x-ray vision; lab coat allows for travel through time and space.

Origin: Since birth, Max Axiom seemed destined for greatness. His mother, a marine biologist, taught her son about the mysteries of the sea. His father, a nuclear physicist and volunteer park ranger, schooled Max on the wonders of earth and sky.

One day on a wilderness hike, a megacharged lightning bolt struck Max with blinding fury. When he awoke, Max discovered a newfound energy and set out to learn as much about science as possible. He traveled the globe earning degrees in every aspect of the field. Upon his return, he was ready to share his knowledge and new identity with the world. He had become Max Axiom, Super Scientist.

Calorie (KA-luh-ree) — a measurement of the amount of energy that food gives you

electromagnetic radiation (i-lek-troh-mag-NET-ik ray-dee-AY-shuhn) — electromagnetic waves of all different lengths; electromagnetic radiation ranges from short gamma rays to long radio waves.

electron (i-LEK-tron) — a tiny particle in an atom that travels around the nucleus

generator (JEN-uh-ray-tur) — a machine that makes electricity by turning a magnet inside a coil of wire

gravity (GRAV-uh-tee) — a force that pulls objects with mass together; gravity pulls objects down toward the center of earth.

insulation (in-suh-LAY-shun) — a material that stops heat, sound, or cold from entering or escaping

joule (JOOL) — a unit of work or energy

kinetic energy (ki-NET-ik EN-ur-jee) — the energy of a moving object

molecule (MOL-uh-kyool) — the atoms making up the smallest unit of a substance

potential energy (puh-TEN-shuhl EN-ur-jee) — the stored energy of an object that is raised, stretched, or squeezed

radiation (ray-dee-AY-shuhn) — a form of energy, such as heat, light, X-rays, microwaves, or radio waves; radiation also includes dangerous, high-energy nuclear radiation.

resistance (ri-ZISS-tuhnss) — a force that opposes or slows the motion of an object; friction is a form of resistance.

READ MORE

Fullick, Ann. *Turning Up the Heat: Energy.* Everyday Science. Chicago: Heinemann, 2005.

McLeish, Ewan. *Energy Crisis.* Talking Points. Mankato, Minn.: Stargazer Books, 2008.

Morgan, Sally. *From Windmills to Hydrogen Fuel Cells: Discovering Alternative Energy.* Chain Reactions. Chicago: Heinemann, 2007.

Sohn, Emily. *A Crash Course in Forces and Motion with Max Axiom, Super Scientist.* Graphic Science. Mankato, Minn.: Capstone Press, 2007.

Woodford, Chris. *Energy.* DK See for Yourself. New York: DK Publishing, 2007.

INTERNET SITES

FactHound offers a safe, fun way to find educator-approved Internet sites related to this book.

Here's what you do:

1. Visit *www.facthound.com*
2. Choose your grade level.
3. Begin your search.

This book's ID number is 9781429623377.

FactHound will fetch the best sites for you!

INDEX